Financial Reporting

The Ultimate Guide to Creating Financial
Reports and Performing Financial Analysis

Contents

INTRODUCTION.. 1

BREAKING DOWN THE BASICS 3

SUMMARY OF THE FOUR MAIN FINANCIAL DOCUMENTS................. 9

INTERNAL VS EXTERNAL FINANCIAL REPORTING............................14

HOW TO ASSESS A FINANCIAL REPORT AS A WHOLE 16

FOOTNOTES: WHAT THEY ARE AND WHY THEY ARE IMPORTANT
....19

HOW TO CREATE AND ANALYZE A FINANCIAL REPORT 21

WHAT IS INCLUDED IN THE FOOTNOTES? 40

WHAT PROGRAMS ARE THERE TO HELP YOU CREATE A
FINANCIAL REPORT 46

SECURITIES AND EXCHANGE COMMISSION (SEC)............................52

QUARTERLY AND ANNUAL REPORTS FOR STOCKHOLDERS 59

PRESS RELEASES AND CONFERENCE CALLS; WHY ARE THEY
IMPORTANT?..62

CONCLUSION 65

Introduction

The concept of this book might seem overwhelming; however, the point of it is to help you grasp what financial reporting and analysis are. Moreover, how to break down the steps to create a financial report that is easy to understand whether you have zero experience and are struggling to find a place to start, or if you already have some knowledge on the topic but are trying to fine-tune your skills.

This book begins with the basics and progresses from there. With each section, you will become more knowledgeable and confident in your ability to take on the task of performing a financial analysis or creating a financial statement.

Understanding a financial report may seem complicated, but once you break it down into manageable parts, the basics are relatively uncomplicated. You just have to get past the jargon and complex formulas that don't convey information any better than just speaking plainly. So that is precisely what this book is going to do. It will break down the jargon using words and concepts that anyone can understand.

It will walk you through the primary documents that are included in a financial report and explain each one in turn. Not only will it explain what each report is, but it will also discuss how to assess the information and what it means. Then, it will show you basic examples of how to create each one without overcomplicating the process.

Although you don't need to be in a position required to create a financial report to reap the benefits this book includes, the layout of the book allows you to either read it from start to finish or skip to whichever area you think is the most pertinent to your needs.

Aside from the breakdown of the income statements, balance sheets, shareholder's equity reports and cash flow statements, you will learn about the differences in quarterly and annual reports, press releases and conference calls and what information they can provide for you. The book will go into detail about the Securities and Exchange Commission and the different types of software that can help you during the process, indicating the advantages and disadvantages of each one.

By the time you finish reading, you will feel more confident in your knowledge and ability to create and analyze a financial report, have a better understanding of the different rules and regulations for businesses and companies in regards to reporting their finances, and acquire knowledge and understanding behind some of the terms that are frequently used within the finance industry as a whole.

Breaking Down the Basics

The term 'financial report' is a generalized compilation of numerous financial statements and pieces of information such as balance sheets, statements of the owners' equity, cash flows and income, to name a few. If you don't know what these things are, don't worry; this book breaks down each one.

The point of a financial report is to show if the business or company can meet all of their operating payments, debt commitments, and potential growth while maintaining service levels, known as the financial viability of a company. Or put simply, a financial report is generated to help assess if a business is making money or not.

The information included in a business' financial report will tell you how much money the business has, how much debt there is, how much money it is bringing in each month and how that money is being spent. The information is shared with the public, including any current or potential lenders and shareholders who are considered to be involved with the business. It will also relay information about a company's financial stability and profitability.

Since both current and potential investors have stakes in how well the business does, it is vital that they know how the business is doing as well as how the company may fair in the future. If a business' financial report speculates that it will struggle in the future, an investor may choose to put their money elsewhere, even if the report shows the business is currently doing ok.

After all, it is only fair that the people who are investing, or who are lenders to a company, should know if their money is being put to good use and will return a profit. If it's not, then it turns into a one-sided relationship with the investor as the losing partner. In other words, a financial report helps an investor assess the risk involved with any company they may be considering contributing to.

Investors and lenders are examples of who can benefit from the knowledge contained in a financial report. Business owners and managers use financial reports to make decisions that will affect the continuation of operations. A financial analysis of the financial statements within the report is then conducted to help the management teams understand the details of the figures. This will also be included in the business' annual reports to its stockholders.

Different statements within a company's financial report can help a labor-union representative or individual employees understand the status of the company's financial health or economic standing. The information can then be used to strengthen an argument for better pay wages, benefits, promotions, working conditions and much more if the data shows that the business is doing well and making a profit.

Financial institutions such as banks or lending companies will assess a company's financial reports when deciding if they want to grant a request for more funds for an expansion or to approve an extension of a debt.

Each of these listed parties will assess different aspects of the report, but every report should be able to answer the following questions:

- Where did the business get its capital from and how is it making use of the money?

- Is the business making a profit or is it suffering a loss and how much?

- How do the business' assets compare to its liabilities?

- How much is the cash flow from the loss or profit for the period?

- Does the business have enough capital to grow in the future?

- Did the business reinvest all of its profit, and if not, where did it go?

The answers to these questions help determine the basics of a company's current and future success allowing all parties to assess how involved they want to be, what risks they want to take concerning the business, and the company's potential achievements or losses.

It would seem that a financial report would be the all-encompassing truth behind how well a business is doing. And although that is the primary purpose, there are a few ways that a company can lie on its financial statement to make it appear that it is doing better than it actually is.

For example, the typical consensus of assessing the profit of a company is by looking at the accrual concept (making sure the company's revenue is more than its expenses); however, within the Generally Accepted Accounting Principles (GAAP), there are many ways to recognize revenue. Depending on which way a company chooses to report, the outcome of the financial statements may look completely different; even though, technically, the economic reality is the same.

For revenue (profit) to be recognized, the company needs to complete the earning process and have no obligation remaining to its customer. In other words, if a company has a deal to produce a shipment of goods to a customer and has only partly delivered the shipment, then the company cannot consider the deal as a profit until the order is complete.

The same thing applies if a company offers a product that comes with a warranty. They cannot count the sale as revenue unless the costs of providing the warranty have been estimated, such as the cost of labor to fix the product, the parts that might be needed, or until the window of the warranty has been closed (if the product has a three-year warranty, the sale cannot be counted as revenue until the three years are completed). Additionally, if the company provides the goods before payment from the consumer, they cannot count it as revenue.

There are four main ways for companies to report revenue.

The first method is <u>sales basis</u>. This is the method that most investors will easily make sense of. It's the most straightforward concept regarding a form of profit. It is when money is exchanged for a good at the time of a sale. The sale can be made with either cash or credit (known as accounts receivable) – like when you go to the store and purchase a shirt you exchange money for the product.

However, the revenue received cannot be recognized if the exchange has occurred before the transaction is complete. Let's say your fitness center sells an annual membership for $600; they will only recognize $50 of revenue every month until the full year of services has been completed. The reason for this is that if they went out of business, they would need to refund a prorated portion of the annual membership to the customer since it had not yet fulfilled the services for which it had been paid.

Some companies take longer to provide their product to their customers. If someone hires a construction company to build a new building, obviously that building won't be completed overnight. However, the construction company will want to show its investors that it is generating a profit even if the project hasn't been officially completed yet.

To do this, they would use the second method, <u>percentage of completion</u>. For the company's revenue to be recognized two conditions need to be met: first, there is a legal, long-term binding contract; and second, it is possible to estimate a percentage of the project as it is completed as well as any future revenues and costs.

There are two ways a percentage of completion method can occur in this sense. One way would be to use milestones, such as laying the foundations and building the framework. If the construction company is paid $100,000 for building a fifteen-unit apartment complex and it takes ten steps to complete the building (breaking ground, excavations, laying the foundations, etc.) they may consider $10,000 per completed step as revenue. The other way would be to see what the total cost of the project is compared to the cost incurred. With this method, the construction company would compare the cost it actually takes to complete the apartment complex to the estimated total cost. In other words, if the company estimated it would take $80,000 out of the $100,000 to complete the project, including labor, parts, equipment, etc., but find after the first month, it only uses $5,000. $5,000 is 6.25% of the estimated $80,000; therefore, they would then multiply the original $100,000 (the total revenue) by the percentage of the incurred cost (6.25% or $6,250) and claim this amount as the revenue on their income statement.

The third method is called the cost recovery. This is used when a company cannot accurately estimate the cost required to complete their project. Let's say a company spends $1,000,000 to develop a software program to help it operate more effectively. Then it decides to sell this software to other companies who could benefit from it for $250,000. They would need to sell the software four times to break even with the expense it took to create it (i.e., $1,000,000). If they were able to sell the software a fifth time, they could report $250,000 as profit. This method is generally considered the most conservative.

The last method is called installment. This occurs when the collection of cash is dependent on a consumer's agreement to pay for a good or service in broken up payments. This happens during real estate transactions where the sale is made, but the collection of cash is dependent on the buyer following through with the financing. An example of this is if a buyer commits to purchasing a property for $500,000 and agrees to pay the full amount in two installments of $250,000 – once upon the agreement of sale, and once six months later. Upon receiving the first payment, the seller would reflect 50% of the revenue and gross profit since he has only collected 50% of the money.

Now that you understand the different ways a company can report its revenue, let's take a look at the other items that are typically found in a financial report, then we will break down each one further to look at how to analyze and create each one. As previously mentioned, the four basic statements are the balance sheet, income statement, cash flow statement, and the shareholders' equity statement.

Summary of the Four Main Financial Documents

Balance Sheet

Below you will see an example of a balance sheet from Accounting Play:

Balance sheet example

TEDDY FAB INC.
BALANCE SHEET
December 31, 2100

ASSETS			LIABILITIES AND SHAREHOLDERS' EQUITY		
Current assets			Current liabilities		
Cash and cash equivalents	$	100,000	Accounts payable	$	30,000
Accounts receivable		20,000	Notes payable		10,000
Inventory		15,000	Accrued expenses		5,000
Prepaid expense		4,000	Deferred revenue		2,000
Investments		10,000	Total current liabilities		47,000
Total current assets		149,000			
			Long-term debt		200,000
Property and equipment			Total liabilities		247,000
Land		24,300			
Buildings and improvements		250,000	Shareholders' Equity		
Equipment		50,000	Common stock		10,000
Less accumulated depreciation		(5,000)	Additional paid-in capital		20,000
			Retained earnings		197,100
Other assets			Treasury stock		(2,000)
Intangible assets		4,000			
Less accumulated amortization		(200)	Total liabilities and shareholders' equity	$	472,100
Total assets	$	472,100			

Above is a very simplified version of what you may see when looking at a company's balance sheet. At times this report can be dozens or even hundreds of pages long depending on the size of the company. It is easy to stare at the columns of numbers and not know what they mean or where to begin.

The purpose of a balance sheet is to tell investors how much money or how many assets a company has, how many liabilities it has (how much it owes), and the remaining amount when you net the two together. In short, it provides a snapshot of what a company owns, owes, and the amount that is invested by shareholders.

Income Statement

Below is an example of an income statement from Investing Answers:

Income Statement for Company XYZ, Inc.
for the year ended December 31, 2008

Total Revenue	$100,000	100.00%
Cost of Goods Sold	($58,473)	-58.47%
Gross Profit	**$41,527**	41.53%
Operating Expenses:		
Salaries	$11,256	11.26%
Rent	$10,009	10.01%
Utilities	$2,250	2.25%
Depreciation	$5,000	5.00%
Total Operating Expenses	$28,515	28.52%
Operating Profit (EBIT)	**$13,012**	13.01%
Interest Expense	($10,000)	-10.00%
Earnings before Tax (EBT)	$3,012	3.01%
Taxes	$1,084	1.08%
Net Income	**$4,096**	4.10%

An income statement is a report that shows how much money a company has made or lost by looking at the income, expenses and the resulting profits or losses of a business at any one time. It calculates the total net income of a company by subtracting the total expenses from the total income. This report is typically the first financial statement used during the accounting cycle because whatever the net income or loss is, it must be carried over to the statement of shareholder's equity before any of the other financial statements can be prepared.

Cash Flow Statement

The following is a sample of a cash flow statement provided by Vertex42:

	[Company Name]		
	Cash Flow Statement		
	For the Year Ending	12/31/2008	
	Cash at Beginning of Year	15,700	

Operations

Cash receipts from customers		693,200
Cash paid for		
Inventory purchases		(264,000)
General operating and administrative expenses		(112,000)
Wage expenses		(123,000)
Interest		(13,500)
Income taxes		(32,800)
Net Cash Flow from Operations		**147,900**

Investing Activities

Cash receipts from		
Sale of property and equipment		33,600
Collection of principal on loans		
Sale of investment securities		
Cash paid for		
Purchase of property and equipment		(75,000)
Making loans to other entities		
Purchase of investment securities		
Net Cash Flow from Investing Activities		**(41,400)**

Financing Activities

Cash receipts from		
Issuance of stock		
Borrowing		
Cash paid for		
Repurchase of stock (treasury stock)		
Repayment of loans		(34,000)
Dividends		(53,000)
Net Cash Flow from Financing Activities		**(87,000)**

Net Increase in Cash		**19,500**
	Cash at End of Year	35,200

© 2008 Vertex42 LLC   Templates by Vertex42.com

11

A cash flow statement indicates where the money was brought in (cash inflow) from and also where the money is being spent (cash outflow). This statement is used in conjunction with the income statement and balance sheet and usually breaks down the company's cash flow into three main categories, including investing in financing activities and operations. We will go into further details about these categories later.

Owners' Equity/Stockholders Equity

Below is an example of a stockholders' equity report from Principles of Accounting:

PEPPER CORPORATION Statement of Stockholders' Equity For the Year Ending December 31, 20X9				
	Common Stock, $1 Par	Paid-in Capital in Excess of Par	Retained Earnings	Treasury Stock	Total Stockholders' Equity
Balance on January 1	$20,000,000	$25,000,000	$11,000,000	$(5,000,000)	$51,000,000
Issued shares for cash	3,000,000	12,000,000			15,000,000
Purchase of treasury stock				(2,000,000)	(2,000,000)
Net income			4,000,000		4,000,000
Cash dividends			(1,500,000)		(1,500,000)
Stock dividends	1,150,000	4,600,000	(5,750,000)		
Balance on December 31	$24,150,000	$41,600,000	$ 7,750,000	$(7,000,000)	$66,500,000

Regarding a corporation, you should know that 'stockholders' equity', 'shareholders' equity' and 'owner's equity' can be interchangeable. If the company is considered a sole proprietorship, the term owner's equity is the most accurate – since, in that case, there are no stockholders. The word equity is the amount stake shareholders have in a company and is measured by accounting rules.

In accounting terms, equity is always the assets minus its liabilities. It is also the total of all capital paid in by shareholders, plus any profits that were earned by the company since it started, minus any dividends that were paid out to shareholders. It is usually the second report found within the financial statement and shows all the changes that have occurred to the owner's equity during the specific period. It further provides more information about the equity related activities throughout a reporting period, and is considered useful for revealing stock repurchasing and sales.

As seen above, it is typically laid out like a grid, with the starting balance in each factor of equity shown across the top, while the middle consists of any changes subtracting or additions from the beginning throughout the reporting time period and ends with balances reflecting the additions and subtractions. For consistency, the same format is recommended for all financial periods.

(Shareholders' equity can be figured out by using this simple equation: Assets – Liabilities = shareholders' equity.)

It is pertinent to state that there are two forms of regulations to follow regarding what is required to be included in all of these statements (and more).

The first is the Generally Accepted Accounting Principles, otherwise known as (GAAP). GAAP represents a combination of standards created by various policy boards and designed to allow investors to assess useful information during their decision-making process by ensuring a minimum level of consistency throughout a company's financial statements. The role of GAAP is to make sure that all financial reporting provided by a company is transparent, easy to read, and consistent from one organization to another. It should be noted that there is no universal standard and it may vary slightly from one geographic location to another within various industries.

The second set of standards comes from an independent federal government agency called the U.S. Securities and Exchange Commission (SEC). The agency is responsible for maintaining an orderly and fair functioning of the securities market and protects investors by ensuring all prevalent information is disclosed in the financial documents. Further detail about the SEC is provided after the rundown of how to create each of the above-described documents. You will see references to both throughout this book, so it is important to understand what they are.

Internal vs External Financial Reporting

The balance sheet and the income statement are prepared for both internal and external use. Internal reports are used within a business or company, and utilized by management to assess where the business is at and to help with any big decisions about where the business should go or how it can improve. Whereas external reports are for external parties such as government and credit institutions or shareholders. These reports will help them assess the risk that is involved with investing or helping the business.

For further understanding, let us take a look at each report individually:

An internal balance sheet is used to report what the financial condition of the business is. This includes more detailed information compared to the external balance sheet. Having greater detail within the internal balance sheet allows for better analysis, control, and help management to make well-informed decisions.

An external balance sheet doesn't usually include quite as much detail; it only includes the financial assets and liabilities. External balance sheets must be classified as short-term liabilities and assets. Because of this, they are also often referred to as 'classified balance sheets'; however, the word 'classified' does not mean top secret or restricted, but rather that the assets and liabilities are sorted into basic classes or groups such as short-term and long-term liabilities. Grouping them in this way helps readers compare and understand the report.

An internal income statement is used to gauge the ability of a company to generate revenue. This statement is used within the company and is not for public knowledge. It does not have to adhere to any formal legal formula or presentation style and can be for any department within a company to help provide a clear financial picture so a company can accurately decide which areas within its infrastructure need improvement.

An external income statement can differ greatly from the internal statement. As stated, the internal income statement does not need to follow any specific guidelines whereas the external income statement does. These statements follow the rules of GAAP which was placed by the U.S. government. By requiring companies to report under these standards, it helps ensure that outside parties get an accurate picture of a company's financial status without the need to know too many details about the company's internal operations.

How to Assess a Financial Report as a Whole

When you are looking at a financial report, it can seem difficult to know what to look at first. Each financial report is going to look a bit different even though they all have the same relative information. If you are looking at an annual report for a public company, you may find that it contains a lot of information, including a highlighted section or a trending chart. It may have extensive footnotes in the financial statements and possibly a lot of propaganda. On the other hand, most private companies will have significantly smaller financial reports containing some footnotes in the financial statement but not much more.

So when looking at a larger report, it is easy to get a bit lost in the information. Sometimes you could look at just the highlights section and a letter from the chief executive to their shareholders – if there is one. Ideally, this letter would summarize an even-handed and modest explanation of the main developments throughout the year; although, these letters often include a shift of blame for a poor performance and are often full of self-congratulatory comments. It is important to read them but take everything with a grain of salt.

Reading the portions mentioned above of the report, they may be good for a general overview of the standing within the company, but for serious investors, it won't be detailed enough. To get a true look at how a company, sub-business, or project is doing, you want to assess the viability, stability, and profitability. To do this, you want to take a close look at the primary documents discussed in this book – the balance sheet, financial report, cash flow report and shareholders' equity statement.

For a business to make a profit, it needs to keep its overall expenses below the amount it makes in sales. Because of this, the best place to look at first is not the bottom line, but the top line, which is where the sales revenue figure is listed. Once you see what that number is, you then want to look at the rest of the document and answer these three questions:

1. What is the gross margin ratio of the business? (you will know how to find this answer when we cover how to analyze income statements).

2. How does sales revenue in the most recent year compare to previous years?

3. Based on the information in the most recent income statement, how do the gross margin and the bottom line (net earnings) compare with its top line (sales revenue)?

When trying to assess the profitability of a company, you need to look at more than just the total profit number for the period. Under the total profit number for public companies is a line that shows the earnings per share (EPS). This is the amount of the bottom line revenue for every share of the company's stock. A private company may not have this line included because they are not required to report it, but you can easily figure it out by dividing its bottom line net income by the amount of ownership shares it holds.

The EPS is important for individual investors because they know it is the primary driver of the market value of their investment with the business. The higher the number, the higher the market value is for a public company and the higher the book value per share is for a private company.

One would think that income statements should be relatively straightforward, but often that is not the case. They may start out showing the sales revenue as less than the expenses of operating the business or making sales, but then you may see a layer of unusual gains and losses as you look further down to the final profit line. This could mean several things; it could mean there was a building that was flooded or potentially a lawsuit. So now what?

Unfortunately, there is no easy answer. On the one hand, you could dismiss it as a rare occurrence, and thus chalk it up to an unforeseen circumstance that couldn't be avoided and therefore assume it is a nonrecurring issue. However, if you look at other financial reports from other periods, you may find the unusual gains and losses reports more regularly which can be a red flag for how a business runs.

Another thing you will want to check is the cash flow from profit. A business' objective is not to just have a profit, but to generate cash flow from that profit as quickly as possible. This is the most important stream of cash inflow to a business. It could be relatively easy to show that a business has profit if they sell off some assets or borrow money. It would technically show a profit, but for a business to stay profitable, it needs to have the cash flow from making profits to make cash distributions to shareholders, to supplement other sources of capital, and to maintain liquidity (available liquid assets) to grow the business.

However, you are not going to find the number of cash inflow sales or the cash outflow of expenses in the income statement. For this reason, do not think the bottom line is a cash flow number. The net cash flow from its sales and expenses is reported in the statement of cash flows, so that is where you want to look.

While looking over the financial report, you are going to want to look for signs of financial distress. It is possible for a business to have a good sales volume and even good profit margins, but if it can't pay its bills on time, they are going to have problems down the road. For this reason, you're going to want to look at the business' history of being able to meet its liabilities and debts on time and in full (known as its solvency). By performing a solvency analysis, you want to look for signs that a business may be in some financial distress that could cause some disruption in their ability to make future profit.

Footnotes: What They Are and Why They Are Important

Many times there is quite a bit of information that is not disclosed on a report because it may not be required to be included by the regulatory authorities. To get a better understanding, you want to look at the footnotes of a financial statement to evaluate the company's financial performance properly.

You will find footnotes included throughout the financial statements. Sometimes they are quite long and in-depth and generally refer to how a company arrived at its figures, the accounting methodologies used for reporting and recording transactions, stock option compensation, pension plans, or any irregularities or inconsistencies within the report. Footnotes are not included in the main report because they can be quite long, and if they were included, they could cloud the data within the financial statement.

Footnotes provide an opportunity for a company to explain its numbers and helps provide some clarity to anyone who is reading the financial statement. They are also usually quite detailed and may reveal issues with a company or business' underlying financial health.

While looking at the footnotes, there are two things you want to focus on.

First is what kind of accounting method the company uses and if it follows the generally accepted accounting method within the industry standards. If the company is using a different accounting method that is not commonly seen compared to others in the industry, or if it seems more aggressive, this may be a sign that it's trying to cover up an event. Or it's trying to give the perception of having a better performance than it really has by manipulating the financial statements.

The second item to assess is if any changes occurred in an account from one financial period to the next, and what kind of effect it will have on the bottom line. To follow these two rules of advice, you must have a basic understanding of what the GAAP standards are. Knowing this will help you realize when a company is possibly trying to cover something up by not using the standard methods.

Financial statements within an annual report are supposed to be relatively easy to read and have a clean appearance, and often other calculations are put into the footnotes. Some examples might be any legal cases the company is/was involved in, errors in previous accounting statements, or details of any synthetic leases (when an entity established by a parent company purchases an asset, then leases it back to the parent company).

However, one of the biggest things to look for is what's not included in the financial report. When a company follows the accounting standards, it is possible for the company to leave a major liability off of the main portion of the report and instead allow them only to report it within the footnotes.

A red flag while looking at the footnotes is if it is very difficult to read and is filled with technical accounting terms and legal jargon or if the footnotes only contain paragraphs on a major issue or event. This is typically done to try and confuse the readers.

How to Create and Analyze a Financial Report

At this point, you should have a solid, generalized understanding of what a financial report is. But knowing what it is and knowing how to analyze or create one are two different things. The purpose behind analyzing a financial report is to evaluate whether a business is stable, profitable (liquid), or solvent enough to warrant a monetary investment. It can also be used to evaluate economic trends, build long-term plans for a business, set financial policies, and identify projects or companies for investments.

Balance Sheet

To start, let's look at the balance sheet. This can be broken down into four components: the assets, the liabilities, the equities and the ratios.

First, you want to know what resources are owned by the company. These are called the assets. The definition of an asset is a property that a person or company owns that is regarded as having monetary value. An example may be land, buildings or machines. These would be considered as long-term assets because they are things that are not intended to be turned into cash but can be sold for a monetary value if needed.

The numbers that go along for long-term assets will tell you what they were worth at the start of the year (or when they were purchased) and what they are worth by the end of the year (after the deduction for depreciation of use.) These numbers are important to know in case the company needs to sell them.

There are also the current assets which are accounts receivables, cash, and prepaid expenses. These are basically the lifeline to keep the daily operations of the company going. The company needs to keep the cash flowing, so it has enough to fulfill demand. Without these, a company can't function. So knowing if there is a shortage of current assets, the company will need to figure out new methods to improve their financial situation.

The liabilities are on the opposite side of the balance sheet. Liabilities are the debts the company will have to pay to creditors, the accounts payable, accrued income taxes from the previous year, repayments on commercial paper, and any other accrued liabilities. There are also the long-term liabilities like monitory debt, capital leases, and any other loan or interest repayments. A company will need to have the ability to back their creditors, so ideally, these numbers need to be within a manageable limit.

Equity is the capital that the owners of the company and other shareholders have invested. Some companies choose to have all their shares owned by promoters, while others have their shares purchased by the general public and freely traded in the market, known as stocks. The numbers are split up into common stock and preferred stock. (Common stockholders generally have voting rights within the company whereas preferred stockholders do not.) They tell the company how many shares (or dividends) they will have to pay and what the voting rights of the members are during their annual meeting. They will also look at the accumulated net income, otherwise known as retained earnings, so they know how much investment has been put back into the company.

Reading a balance sheet can help derive a number of ratios that will help investors get a sense of how healthy a company is. An example of this would be the fixed asset turnover ratio. This is usually one of the biggest numbers listed on the report and often represents the largest component of a company's assets. A "fixed asset" is also known as property, plant, and equipment (PP&E). You can get the fixed asset turnover ratio by simply dividing the year-end PP&E of two fiscal periods. Keep in mind, the number of fixed assets is largely dependent on the line of business. Some businesses require more fixed assets than others. Service-based companies or computer software producers generally need a smaller amount of fixed assets compared to mainstream manufacturers.

The <u>return on assets ratio</u> (ROA) is another example. This one shows how many total assets a company is earning. You can get this number by dividing the total year-end assets of the two fiscal periods. An ROA is shown as a percentage return (an investment of loss or gain over a specific period which is then expressed as a percentage). A high percentage return suggests well-managed assets.

There is another sneaky form of assets. These are called the intangible assets, which can be separated into three different types: intellectual property (or copyrights, patents, brand names, etc.), purchased goodwill (the cost of an investment in excess of book value), and deferred charges (known as, capitalized expenses). Unfortunately, it can be difficult to always include these types of assets because more often than not, they are intangible or are buried among other assets and are typically only disclosed in a note within the financial footnotes.

While analyzing a balance sheet, keep in mind that the information provided is to assess the basics of how a business is doing only during a specific period. To get a real idea of how a business is doing based on this report, you may want to compare it to previous periods of the business.

Now that you know what a balance sheet is and how it is used let's take a look at how you can create one. Below is a template example provided by QuickBooks. You can refer to this image throughout the instruction breakdown to help you make sense of the steps:

	Current [Date]	Forecast [Date]		Current [Date]	Forecast [Date]
ASSETS			**LIABILITIES**		
Current Assets			Current Liabilities		
Checking Account	$	$	Accounts Payable	$	$
Accounts Receivable			Business Credit Cards		
Prepaid Insurance			Operating Line of Credit		
Inventory			Sales Tax Payable		
			Payroll Liabilities		
Fixed Assets					
Furniture and Equipment			Long-term Liabilities		
(Accum Dep. - Furniture)			Car Loan Payable		
Computer Equipment			Business Loan		
(Accum Dep. - Computers)			Shareholder's Loan		
Vehicles					
(Accum Dep. - Vehicles)					
Buildings			EQUITY		
(Accum Dep. - Buildings)			Opening Balance Equity		
Land			Capital Stock		
			Dividends Paid		
			Owners Draw		
Other Assets			Retained Earnings		
Patents					
Other Investments					
Other Assets					
TOTAL ASSETS	$	$	**TOTAL LIABILITIES & EQUITY**	$	$

A simplified version of an equation your balance sheet should be able to answer is this:

Liabilities + Owner's Equity = Assets

And just like any math equation, you should be able to change the variables around to isolate one category. To calculate the company's equity, most business owners or investors may use an equation like this:

Assets – Liabilities = Owner's Equity

Step two is to calculate the assets. All assets, investments, products of the business and money that the company possesses can be converted into cash. This number is what puts companies in the financial positive. A sign of a healthy company is if its total assets are greater than the sum of its liabilities.

You want to list the assets by their liquidity (the amount of cash the asset is worth). Once you know the numbers, you want to list them starting with cash itself first and then relaying long-term investments at the end of the list. If you are creating an annual balance sheet, you will want to separate the assets into two groups: the current assets and fixed assets.

Once you have made your list, you are ready to start step three which is to determine the company's liabilities. As per the above-listed equation, the liabilities are the negative numbers. These may include the operational costs, material expenses, or debt. In general, the lower this number is, the better. These too can be separated into two lists: 'current liabilities' and 'fixed liabilities'.

Now, let's take a closer look at this equation:

Assets – Liabilities = Owner's Equity

This will show you the value of the company's capital. If the answer to this equation is a negative net worth, it can be dangerous, especially for small businesses, and could cause issues for them to secure financing. If it shows a positive net worth, it shows the business owners have the options of getting more capital by selling part of their business off in stocks, equity, or dividends.

After you complete these steps, you should have something along the lines of the above illustration. Remember, this is just a basic understanding of how to create a balance sheet and the assets and/or liabilities may vary based on the specific industry and size of the business.

Statement of Stockholders' Equity

Stockholders' equity, also known as shareholders' equity, consists of shared capital plus the retained earnings and is typically found on a company's balance sheet. When we talked about the balance sheet, we mentioned the equations of Liabilities + Owner's Equity = Assets. Or Assets – Liabilities = Owner's Equity. For this section, we are going to substitute 'Owner' for 'Shareholder' – the only difference between the two, as previously mentioned, is an owner would refer to a sole business owner with a sole proprietorship, whereas a shareholder refers to a larger company or business.

An easy way to understand these equations can be found in the image below provided by the Corporate Finance Institute (CFI):

Stockholders' Equity

Assets		Contributed Capital
–	or	+
Liabilities		Retained Earnings

The point of the statement of shareholder's equity is to show the changes in equity from the beginning of an accounting period to the end of one. Moreover, it displays all equity accounts, such as the common stock, net income, dividends, and paid in capital, which affects the ending equity balance. Put simply; it is an in-depth view of how the equity balance for a company on January 1 turned into the equity balance the company has on December 31.

While reading a shareholder's equity statement, it usually includes at least six different components. It is usually the second document created within the financial report and is usually issued as part of the balance sheet.

The first component shows the preferred stock. Someone with a preferred stock would also have an ownership stake in the company. It offers holders a higher claim on a company's assets or earning compared to those who have common stock. Preferred stockholders are usually entitled to receive their dividends before common stockholders do. They do not have voting rights within the company, and their stock is usually listed at face value (or par value), which means the amount that it is redeemable.

Common stock means the shareholder has voting rights in corporate decision-making. They are lower on the list of priorities when it comes to paying the equity holders. Moreover, if a company needs to liquidate, they are not paid out until after the preferred stockholders and the bondholders. Although similar to preferred stock, common stock is also shown on the statement of shareholders' equity at face value.

A company may repurchase its own stock to boost its stock price or as an attempt to avoid a takeover; in this case, the stock would be referred to as a Treasury Stock. A shareholder's equity would be reduced by the amount of money that was spent to repurchase the shares in question.

Contributed capital, also known as additional paid capital, is the excess amount that investors have paid over the par value (face value) of a company's stock.

The total amount of earnings a company has brought in that haven't been distributed to shareholders yet is called retained earnings. To get this number, you subtract the amount paid out from a shareholders' dividends from the company's total earnings since the time the company was created. If a company has been around for a while, this number will probably be on the larger side.

Lastly, is the unrealized gains and loss. This reflects the pricing changes for investments. An unrealized gain happens when an investment gains in value but has not been cashed in, whereas an unrealized loss happens when an investment loses value but has not been sold off yet.

Shareholders will look at this report to see how their investments are doing. However, it is also a useful tool for management within the company to use in helping them make decisions about the future issuances of stock shares.

Below you will see an example of a Statement of Shareholder's Equity provided by Accounting Coach:

This statement seems like it would be complicated to put together, but you are just filling in the boxes. The first line is going

	Common Stock - par	Common Stock - excess of par	Retained Earnings	Accumulated Other Comprehensive Income	Treasury Stock	Total
ABC Corporation						
Statement of Stockholders' Equity						
For the Year Ended December 31, 2017						
Balance, Dec 31, 2016	xxx	xxxx	xxxxx	xxx	(xxx)	xxxxxx
Net earnings			xxxx			xxx
Other comprehensive income				xx		xx
Treasury stock purchases					(x)	(x)
Dividends			(xx)			(xx)
Balance, Dec 31, 2017	xxx	xxxx	xxxxxx	xxxx	(xxxx)	xxxxxx

See accompanying notes to the financial statements.

to be used as the titles of the columns. You will want a column for each stockholders' equity amount. These may include: common stock, paid in capital, preferred stock, common stock, treasury stock, and dividends. You only need to include the ones the company is a part of, but these are the most common. On the far right, you need a 'Total' column or Total Stockholders Equity.

The first row will always be the beginning balance in each account as it stands at the beginning of the year. Remember, the starting amount will always be the same as the ending amount for the previous financial period. Write the name of every stockholders' equity account on the left side of the report, directly under the beginning balance. Then record the amount that appears in each shareholder's equity account. For example, if a company distributed 2,000,000 common shares that have $1 par value, then you would put $2,000,000 under the account of 'issued shares'.

Keep in mind, dividends reduce retained earnings and therefore should have parenthesis around the amount to indicate that they are subtracted from retained earnings. A treasury stock reduces stockholders' equity so it must also have parenthesis around its amount to indicate a negative number.

After you have filled in all the amounts, calculate the total stockholders' equity from the totals column starting at the top of the column which should be the amount from the last period, add the items like net income and issued shares and subtract items like the dividends and treasury stock. This result shows the ending balance total of the shareholders' equity account as of the end of the current financial period.

Income Statement

The income statement is often denoted as the profit and loss statement (P&L) and is one of the most scrutinized financial statements that are issued by every organization. Almost every income statement you look at will be different from the last, although they all include data showing the total revenue, expenses and net income. Technically, that is all that's required to be in the statement. However, the majority of the time there will be additional details within each section to give readers further insight into the company or organization's financial activities.

The following items are the most common line items, and you will typically see them listed in the order below:

- *Product Level Revenue*: this is the revenue associated with a specific product the company sells. If the company or firm sells multiple products, there may be a line for each one.

- *Costs of Goods Sold (or COGS):* this shows the costs that are directly tied to the product – either the ingredients, parts or anything else that goes into creating it.

- *Gross Profit*: this is the profit left over after subtracting the COGSs.

- *Selling, General, and Administrative Expense (SG&A):* this is an accumulation of all costs that are related to the sale of the company's products along with the general operation of the business.

- *Interest Expense*: this shows how much interest the company paid to fund its operation during the period reflected in the statement.

Although there are many metrics and analysis that can be created with this data, when it is used to compare one company with a different but similar company, this information becomes very valuable.

While looking at an income statement, you may notice a few different things. One is that there are hardly any minus signs in front of deductions – if any at all. Usually, these will have parenthesis to indicate a negative number. Although the number itself may not be negative in the terms of below zero, it is considered negative because it is money that a company spends. Therefore, it is the opposite of profit. You may also notice that profit isn't called 'profit'; it is typically referred to as 'net income', 'revenue', 'net earnings' or sometimes just 'earnings'. Also, keep in mind that you want to make sure the sales revenue of goods sold and the cost of goods sold match up so you can get the get the gross profit (the amount of profit before the deductions of other expenses).

To create an Income Statement, we are going to use an example from The Balance shown on the next page.

XYZ Company	
Income Statement	
For the Year Ending Dec 20xx	

1. Sales	$1,000,000
2. Costs of Goods Sold	$500,000
3. Gross Profit	$500,000
4. Selling & Administrative Expense	$250,000
5. Deprecation	$80,000
6. Operating Profit (EBIT)	$170,000
7. Interest	$30,000
8. Earnings Before Taxes (EBT)	$140,000
9. Taxes (21%)	$29,400
10. Earnings Available to Common Shareholders	$110,000
11. Dividends or Owner Draw	$20,000
12. Net Income	$90,600

The example above is a basic template, depending on the size or industry of the particular business, additional lines may need to be included. However, this template includes the basis of what every business will include, and we are going to break down each line:

Line 1: This line shows what the gross revenue is. It is the total dollar amount of sales the business made during the duration for the income statement period. This number includes the amount of total items sold even if the business has not collected the money.

Line 2: The number listed here shows the amount of money a business spent to acquire everything directly related to generating the product it sells. This could include the parts of the product or direct labor costs. This number is often the company's largest expense.

Line 3: When you subtract line 2 (goods sold) from line 1 (gross sales), you get the number listed in line 3 (gross profit).

Line 4: From this example, take the $500,000 of gross profit and subtract the selling and administrative expenses. The resulting $250,000 shows what the office expenses are. These are the costs that do not directly relate to producing goods for sale.

Line 5: When a business purchases something like machinery or a building, it depreciates (loses value) over time. Depreciation acts as a tax shelter and is counted as a non-cash expense. For this reason, it is included in the income statement.

Line 6: Once you have subtracted line 4 (selling and administrative expenses) and line 5 (depreciation amount), you get the amount of the business' operating profit (the amount of earnings before interest and taxes are taken out).

Line 7: After you calculate the EPIT, you will want to add the company's interest expense. To do this, you need to know what the interest rate is on any loans or debt the company has, then take the amount of interest and multiply it by the principal sum of their debt.

Line 8: Take the number for line 7 (interest) and subtract it from line 6 (EBIT) and you arrive at the earnings before taxes which is placed here on line 8.

Line 9: This number is the amount the business or company pays in federal, state, payroll, and local taxes.

Line 10: You should have the proceeds that are available for the business' common shareholders after you have deducted the amount of tax expense, then you will place it here on line 10.

Line 11: You will want to record the dividends here if the business or company has investors or if they take a salary from the company.

Line 12: Now you want to subtract the amounts for all the expenses listed above from line 2 (costs of goods sold) to find out what the net income (profit) is for the company. This number shows how much money the company has left over that they can reinvest into the business.

Once you have arrived at the company's net income, you will want to place it on the balance sheet.

Cash Flow Statement

The purpose of a cash flow statement is to show how a business uses its money, (known as cash outflow) and where the money is coming from (known as cash inflow). It will have three different sections that relate to specific parts of a company's business activities (operations, financing, and investing).

The section about cash flow from operations will show the amount of money from the income statement that had originally been reported on an accrual basis. An example of what might be added here are the accounts payable, income taxes payable, and accounts receivable. Any changes in a company's current assets or liabilities are recorded as cash flow from operations.

Equity and debt transactions are placed in the cash flow from the financing section. If they have a cash flow that would involve repurchased or sale of stocks or bonds, payment of dividends, then this would be counted as cash flow for financing. An example might be if a company used cash to make payments for a long-term debt or received cash from taking out a loan, both of these would be entered in this section. This section is particularly important for investors who prefer dividend-paying companies since instead of showing net income being used to paying its shareholders it shows cash dividends paid.

Cash flow that comes from investing keeps track of the amount that comes from sales or of any purchases of long-term investments like equipment, fixed assets, properties, or land as an example. Usually, investing in transactions generate cash outflow while cash inflow comes from the sales of assets, securities, and businesses. Investors will monitor what a company spends to acquire fixed assets (otherwise known as capital expenditures) that are used to maintain, or any add-ons to a company's physical assets to sustain the company's competitiveness and/or operations. This shows how a company is investing in itself.

Similar to the balance sheet, the cash flow statement can also include several ratios that indicate the quality of investment based on a company's cash flow. One such ratio is called the operating cash flow/net sales. This percentage shows a company's net operating cash flow compared to its revenue (or net sales), which tells us the amount of cash generated from every dollar of their sales. The equation you would want to use is operations cash flow divided by their current liabilities = operating cash flow ratio. You want to look at the cash flow statement to find the cash flow from operations and the amount of current liabilities on the balance sheet. Although there is not a specific percentage to aim for, the higher the number, the better.

Price to cash flow ratio is thought to give a good impression of how a business' value is compared to the earnings ratio. If the company is being traded, then this number is a good one to know since it compares the cash flow the company generates to the company's share price on a per share basis. The equation is as follows: share price divided by the operating cash flow per share = price to cash flow ratio. The share price is typically the final price of the stock on any given day, and operating cash flow is taken from the cash flow statement – although some companies substitute free cash flow with operating cash flow.

Free cash flow is found when you subtract capital expenditures from the net operating cash flow (sometimes known as 'net cash operating activities' or 'operating cash'). This percentage will show you how skilled a company is at creating cash. It is very important to keep an eye on the free cash flow across multiple periods and compare the numbers to other companies within the same industry to get a better feel of how the company is operating. Free cash flow will be considered positive if it shows the company can meet their requirements, including paying its dividends and funding its operating activities.

Free cash flow captures all the good qualities of a company's ability to internally produce cash from its operations while monitoring the cash used for capital expenditures. If the cash flow is a positive number, then it is a clear sign that it's in a good position to prevent excessive borrowing. The company may potentially be able to expand its business, pay its dividends and may make it through a rough patch.

You may have heard of the term 'cash cow'. Although not a typically appealing term, it is a term for companies that have ample free cash flow. It is definitely an appealing trait that investors look for.

Cash flow from operations (average total liabilities), is like total debt to total assets ratio. These would assess the ability of a business to pay its debts, its solvency and its ability to stay afloat. However, this one differs in that it isolates a point in time vs. the ability to measure over a period of time. To get this ratio, you divide the cash flow from operations from the average total liabilities. The number for cash flow from operations will be on the cash flow sheet, whereas the average total liabilities will be on the balance sheet.

The simplest ratio is called the current ratio. This informs the owner if the current assets are good enough to pay their debts. To find it you just take the current assets and divide it by the current liabilities; you can get both of these numbers from the balance sheet.

Lastly, we have the quick ratio, also known as the acid test. This one removes the inventory from the equation and instead measures the business' ability to liquidate if it doesn't have inventory to sell to meet its short-term debt. If the resulting number is less than 1.0, then they will need to sell some inventory to meet their obligations for their short-term debt. This would not be a good spot for a business to be in. To get this ratio, you take the current assets minus inventory (or current liabilities). All numbers should be provided on the balance sheet.

Below is an example of an indirect cash flow statement provided by The Balance:

XYZ Company Statement of Cash Flow

1. Net Income	$110,500
2. Deprecation	$50,000
3. Increase in Accounts Receivable	($30,000)

4. Increase in Inventory	($20,000)
5. Decrease in Prepaid Expenses	$10,000
6. Increase in Accounts Payable	$35,000
7. Decrease in Accrued Expenses	($5,000)
8. Net Cash Flows from Operating Activities	$150,000
9. Increase in Investments	($30,000)
10. Increase in Plant and Equipment	($100,000)
11. Net Cash Flow from Investing Activities	($130,000)
12. Increase in Long-Term Bank Loans	$50,000
13. Dividends Paid	($65,000)
14. Net Cash Flow from Financing Activities	($15,000)
15. Net Increase in Cash Flows	$5,500

The first thing to do when preparing a cash flow statement is to gather the comparative balance sheet and income statement for the corresponding time period, and preferably, the statements for the previous two years. You will need to compare where the company currently is with where it was according to the previous financial statements.

The second thing is to break the information down into three sections. Section one is the cash flows from operations. Section two is cash flow from investing activities. Section three is cash flow from financing activities. We are going to look at the above example starting with section one and work our way down.

To begin, you will want to take the net income and the depreciation amount from the income statement and place it on lines 1 and 2. After that, you will need to asses any decreases or increases in the company's current assets and liability accounts from the previous two years' worth of balance sheets. This number then goes on line 3.

We touched on this before, but please notice line 3 is in parentheses (or a negative number). The reason for this is, in this example, the company extended $30,000 more credit to its customers, so that is $30,000 less than the company has to use. This resulted in a decrease compared to the previous years.

For line 4, you will want to compare how much inventory the company has, and if it increased or decreased its amounts. In this example, it increased by $20,000, whereas line 5 (prepaid expenses) decreased by $10,000. This number is shown as a positive because a decrease in asset accounts means there is more money to fund the business.

The next two lines represent the liabilities sections within the balance sheet. Line 6 shows the amount of their accounts payable has increased by $35,000, for this example. That means the short-term bank loans did not change. Line 7 is for accrued expenses (wages and taxes) which decreased by $5,000. Because this number decreased in a liability account, the company had to use its funds, and therefore this is a negative number.

Line 8 is the summary of the first section of this statement which represents the net cash flow from operating activities. You get this number when you get the total amount of adjustments to the net income and depreciation. In this example, the business is generating positive net cash flow.

The second part is the cash flow from investing activities. This part usually incorporates any long-term investments the company has made and any investments within its fixed assets.

You see that the company invested an increased amount of $30,000 in long-term investments during this period on line 9. This again is shown as a negative number because it was a use of assets. Similarly, line 10 dictates the company spent $100,00 on equipment, etc. This is also shown as a negative number because it was money spent. Net cash flow from investing activities is represented on line 11 and is the summary of the second section of the cash flow statement. You get this by adding lines 9 and 10 together.

Lastly, the third section shows the cash flow from financing activities. With the example we are using, the company has financed their business with long-term bank loans which have increased by $50,000, as you can see on line 12.

The company has also paid $65,000 in dividends to its investors which is a cash outflow, and therefore a negative number as represented on line 13. The difference between lines 12 and 13 will show the net cash flow from financing activities which in this case is $15,000 and a negative number.

Now that all three sections have been laid out for you, you want to combine the final number in each section to see where a business is from a cash flow perspective. The number you get goes on line 15. You will want to make sure this number matches the cash account on the corresponding balance sheet to ensure this is correct. If it is not, you may have made a mistake or miscalculated something along the way.

What is Included in the Footnotes?

You should already know the general reasoning behind the importance of the footnotes within the financial report. Now we are going to go a little further in-depth about what could be included and what you would want to include within the footnotes. This is referring to the footnotes as 'footnotes' but please bear in mind that you may see it referred to as 'explanatory note' or simply just 'note' – but all three of these terms can be used interchangeably.

One of the first things you want to do while deciding what to include is to explain which accounting policies the company or business has chosen to use and why. Along with it, is a little information about the specific company or business – what they do and how they do it. For example, if a company sells a product, do they manufacture it themselves or do they contract it out?

It is important to distinguish which accounting policy the company has chosen to use to enable the reader to understand the financial statements which will, in turn, help the reader evaluate a fair assessment of the financial statement. You will need to explain every significant accounting choice that was made by the company. At the very least, you'll want to explain how a company values its ending inventory, what depreciation methods they have chosen, the type of accounting they used for their income taxes, their basis of consolidation, accounting for intangibles, and information about employee benefits.

As you know, depreciation of asset is the decrease in value of a tangible asset over time after the point of purchase, due to wear and tear, usage or obsolescence. A business values the ending inventory using an inventory valuation method. The methods a company chooses to use for both the depreciation expense and inventory valuation (the value of a company's total inventory at the end of a reporting period) can cause some major fluctuations in the amount of assets that are shown on a balance sheet and the amount of net income shown on the income statement.

There are four main types of methods to assess depreciation.

The first is called straight line. This is a very common, simple way to calculate the expense. It evenly divides the cost of the asset over its useful life. For example, if a company buys a machine for $50,000 and its useful life is estimated at twenty years, the company would divide the $50,000 by twenty, resulting in $2,500 each year.

The second method is called declining balance which is an accelerated method. This method includes a higher depreciation expense during the starting years of the ownership. This method may be used for assets like computers that may not have a very long estimated useful life. To get this number, they would take the net book value (the net value of the asset at the beginning of the accounting period), subtracting the total depreciation amount from the cost of the asset, leaving you with an estimated salvage value at the end of the assets useful life.

The third is the sum of the year's digits which is a little more complicated. This method computes the cost of depreciation by adding up all the expected years of the fixed asset's useful life and compares the total number of years to which year you are currently in.

Lastly, we have the units of production. For this one, take a look at the total number of units (products) the asset is expected to produce throughout its useful life compared to the total amount it produced during the current financial period to calculate the depreciation.

When comparing financial statement figures with another company's figures, it is important to know which methods each company uses. Differences in the net income could be due to depreciation or inventory valuation, but it could also be because of the methodology used. Without the footnote, the reader would never know.

Two inventory issues need to be disclosed in the footnotes. One is the basis upon how the company states their inventory (market or lower of cost), and the other is the method they used to determine the cost. GAAP allows three options for cost flow assumptions.

Weighted average is an average you get from multiplying each component by a factor that reflects its importance. For example, they would take the total cost of the items in inventory that are available for sale and divide it by the total number of units available for sale.

First in, first out (FIFO) is a cost flow based on the assumption that the first goods that are procured are also the first goods sold. The majority of companies believe this presumption comes close to the actual flow of goods, and so is considered the most theoretically accurate inventory valuation method. This method is very similar to the first out, first in (FOFI) which is essentially the same concept except with the assumption that the first goods purchased are the first ones removed from the inventory account.

Specific identification is the tracking and costing of inventory based on the movement of specific inventory items that can actually be considered both in and out of stock. This method is used when individual items can be clearly identified, such as with a stamped receipt date, a serial number, or RFID tag.

Information for both depreciation and inventory is most commonly addressed in the footnotes that provide a summary of the accounting policies.

However, not all assets are tangible. Intangible assets would be something the company owns but can't be touched, like a patent, computer software, a domain name, or trademark. They can be difficult to assign with a monetary value because of the uncertainty of what their future benefits would be, and the useful life can be

and pension plans, including the obligation of the business to pay for health and medical costs of their retired employees.

If a contingent liability exists, it is required to be disclosed if the company will owe a substantial amount of additional interest and tax penalties if the unsolved examination winds up in favor of the government. A contingent liability is when an existing circumstance can cause a loss in the future, depending on events that have not happened yet and may not ever happen. For instance, if a company is involved in an income tax dispute.

Another requirement of the footnotes is to include any claims by creditors against the company's assets. It shows how the company is financing both present and future costs, which gives the reader a look at future cash flows, which can affect the payment of dividends.

What Programs Are There to Help You Create a Financial Report

After reading about everything that goes into creating a financial report you may be wondering how you are supposed to actually be able to complete one – even with the understanding of what goes into creating one. There are endless programs that can assist you or even practically do it for you. Deciding if you should use one or which one to use is no easy task, considering the amount of options that are out there. So here are the best options to help you decide.

The first thing you need to do is decide which features you need in a software so you can choose the exact one or ones that are right for you. Financial software can help you with anything, from simple bookkeeping to complex double entry solutions, forecasting, intuitive analytic observations and more. We are only going to focus on the types of software that will help you create documents like the balance sheet, cash flow, and income statements. Not all software programs will be 100% efficient in creating each of the individual reports so, within the explanation of the software, we are also going to look at which ones are the best for each aspect of the financial report as well.

No one likes to spend unnecessary money, and of course, some programs are available for free online or as part of other software packages. Programs like Microsoft Office Suite and Excel coincide with Google Docs and provide free spreadsheets and templates, but these programs will often require you to do some customization to figure out the layout that would fit you best. However, these programs will only satisfy the basic needs of new business owners or for businesses that are still relatively small.

There are three categories an accounting program can fall within. There is the database software, the installed accounting software, and there's the cloud accounting software. For this book, we aren't going to go into detail about the first two because these options are usually used from within a business or corporation and can cost thousands of dollars along with high maintenance and often the need for multiple system engineers to consultants to set it up. Systems that involve the cloud are relatively easy to use, less expensive, allow you to access the information from anywhere on any device, and lets you send and share your reports just as easily.

Freshbooks is one of the most popular and best cloud-based accounting apps out there. It is designed to help companies handle their finances efficiently and securely. It is used by >5,000,000 customers from all around the world. Its users can take a picture of a receipt or link their bank for fast expense tracking and has won awards for its customer support. However, is it the best option for creating financial statements? According to reviews, although it is a fantastic option for small business owners or freelancers to track their own business, it seems to fall short when it comes to its metrics, reporting features and goal settings. It has a decent platform for creating balance sheets and income statement but falls short with its ability to create a cash flow statement. However, it is considered a cheaper option offering a $15/month membership and has been improving its ability to function for the needs of any sized business.

Zoho Books has become one of the most user-friendly cloud accounting programs for small businesses. Most users love that it allows them to send professionally designed invoices while having reliable support and security. But Zoho Books is more than just a pretty template. It also offers tools that can consolidate accounting tasks like cash flow management, balance sheets, and profit/loss estimates. Although these things are considered typical and standard accounting tasks, it is simple to use, easy to navigate and offers visual charts and quick overviews. Its price makes it a great option for anyone who is just starting out since it's only $9/month at its entry point.

But not everyone is just starting out, and Sage Intacct ERP knows it. This program helps meet the needs of not just small business but also medium-sized businesses that want to level up. This program is great especially for industries like healthcare, retail, and distribution. It allows you to customize reporting based on commissions or any other metric you (or the company) want to be highlighted. It offers the ability to go beyond just accounting and into fixed assets, inventory management, and project management. (Although all of these amazing features come at a pretty hefty entry price of $400.)

FinancialForce Accounting is an all-encompassing program for small businesses to large enterprises and offers more complex financial management needs. It will not only help a business stay on track with its accounts payable and accounts receivable but also its depreciation. It also offers sophisticated reporting tools like balance sheets, income statements, sales reports, and horizontal and vertical analysis. Moreover, it offers modularized package options which would give you more flexible pricing.

However, when you find article after article comparing new and old programs to QuickBooks that says something about the program itself. QuickBooks is a computer program that is generally considered a 'jack-of-all-trades'. It provides a platform that can help you create all four of the primary financial statements within an annual financial report. It will calculate everything for you to help you save time with any manual mathematics which will also prevent any miscalculations that can throw off an entire report. You can create the balance sheet instantly from anywhere, thanks to the cloud. It allows you to customize practically every aspect of your balance sheet, so it only shows the information that the company needs. It is so easy to use that anyone can create one. You don't need to be an accountant to figure it out, and its design makes it easy to share with its ability to email it to anyone from any device.

When it comes to creating an income statement, QuickBooks allows you to choose which method you want to use. Single step method determines net income by subtracting the expenses and losses from gains and revenue. Service-based businesses typically use this method. Another method would be the Multiple step method which separates operating expenses and revenue from other expenses and revenue within the business or company. This will allow you to show the company's gross profit and is an excellent option for businesses based on inventory.

Although the Indirect method is the more popular method of creating a cash flow statement, QuickBooks doesn't limit your options and allows you to choose between direct and indirect. It offers templates and spreadsheets that you can customize to reflect the most optimized layout to fit the company's needs.

QuickBooks even provides the ability to create a Shareholders Equity report (also known as a retained earnings report), along with an owner's equity with templates and educational tools to help you along the way.

QuickBooks is a one-stop shop for anyone from the self-employed to large corporations. They also offer a specialized version based on what your needs are, what the business does, and offers continuing educational material to be kept updated on the newest ideas and concepts within the financial reporting industry. They have four different options to choose from based on your needs and all offer a free trial before purchase. If you find it is the right fit for you, then each has a monthly fee to maintain the membership. In this way, if you that find you no longer need the program or ultimately decide it's not the best fit for you, you can simply discontinue.

Don't go grabbing your phone or computer to purchase one of these programs just yet. Although there are many options out on the market to choose from and there is probably more than one that will meet your needs, you may decide not to use one after all.

It's true that accounting software can save time and help preserve data, but there are some disadvantages to using them as well.

When a person or business is too reliant on accounting software, there may be a loss of data or a work disruption if there is ever a power outage or a service outage. This could prevent any data from being entered and would prevent your access to any data you had saved. Not to mention if you haven't backed it up; you could potentially lose everything

Accounting systems can be excellent at cutting down the amount of manual math involved in creating the income statements, balance sheets or any other financial document, but it is also only as valid as the information that was put into the system. Since most programs require you to at least input the initial figures manually, any typo could result in incorrect information which could lead to trouble down the line. What's worse is if you only review the document once it is completed; you may have a hard time figuring out where the mistake occurred.

Every business is unique and has its own unique needs that must be met. And although many of the programs can be customized, they can only be customized to a certain point and could cause lots of downtime and inaccuracies if it is not customized correctly. Plus, as a business grows, its needs also grow and change which could mean you would need to change to a new program, resulting in the tedious task and wasted time of transferring all of your previously inputted information into a new system. This can also lead to misinformation accidentally inputted, on top of the time it takes to learn the new system.

Information that can be stored electronically can also be manipulated and easily accessed if proper securities and control measures are not put in place. You will need to ensure that strict access controls are set up to make sure that only authorized personnel has access to use the accounting software and reports. It could be extremely dangerous for a company's financial information to end up in the wrong hands and using an accounting software could create the potential for fraud.

One of the biggest downsides is usually the cost involved. Many programs offer a trial period, but once that time is up, you could be hit with skyrocket rates or hidden fees. The basic program itself could be affordable, but some customization, training, maintenance or computer hardware are more than likely additional expenses required to use the program. Sometimes the time savings can justify the costs. For some people and businesses, it could take years before a program pays for itself.

Securities and Exchange Commission (SEC)

Now let's talk about the SEC (Securities and Exchange Commission). Thanks to new technology and apps, the world of investing has opened up to far more people than it reached before. The purpose of the SEC is to aid capital formation, protect investors, and uphold orderly, fair, and efficient markets. This paragraph from their direct website sums it up:

"The laws and rules that govern the securities industry in the United States derive from a simple and straightforward concept: all investors, whether large institutions or private individuals, should have access to certain basic facts about an investment before buying it, and so long as they hold it. To achieve this, the SEC requires public companies to disclose meaningful financial and other information to the public. This provides a common pool of knowledge for all investors to use to judge for themselves whether to buy, sell, or hold a particular security. Only through the steady flow of timely, comprehensive, and accurate information can people make sound investment decisions."

The SEC is an independent government agency tasked to keep public companies in check and accountable for making sure their financial records are available to the public, specifically for investing purposes. It is made up of five commissioners that are appointed by the president of the United States. The president chooses one of the five to be the Chair of the Commission. Each one of them will serve a five-year term. Each term is set up, so one commissioner's term ends on June 5 every year. To make sure the SEC remains unbiased, only a maximum three of the five commissioners can belong to the same political party.

The SEC's headquarters is in Washington DC and is divided into five divisions with twenty-three different offices, eleven of which are also in Washington DC. The five divisions are as follows:

Division of Corporation Finance: They oversee and review documents the SEC require public companies to file, like registration statements, proxy materials, annual reports, and annual and quarterly filings. They provide interpretation of securities acts and provide counseling and guidance to the public and registrants to help them follow the securities laws. The division also scrutinizes the performances of the accounting profession that result in the formulation of GAAP.

Division of Trading and Markets: They oversee the Security Investor Protection Corporation and provides major securities market participants with day-to-day oversight. They assist the SEC in performing its task to keep orderly, fair, and efficient markets. This division also reviews any proposed changes to existing rules and market surveillance.

Division of Investment Management: They protect investors and are held liable for endorsing capital formation via regulation and oversight of the U.S. investment management industry (which includes investment advisers, professional funds managers, mutual funds and research analysts). They ensure that disclosures about popular investment types like exchange funds or mutual funds are useful to retail investors and make sure that there are no excessive amount of regulatory costs that consumers have to pay. They also assist the SEC with giving assistance in enforcement, including businesses and advisers and interpret laws and regulations for the public.

Division of Enforcement: They help the SEC execute its law enforcement in three ways:

1. By recommending the start of investigations into securities law violations;

2. By proposing that the SEC bring civil actions as administrative proceedings or to the federal court before an administrative law judge; and

3. By working closely with law enforcement agencies when needed and prosecuting such cases on behalf of the SEC.

<u>Division of Economic and Risk Analysis:</u> They have two main functions: first, to provide research, analysis, data analytics, and risk assessment to the SEC on issues that present the biggest perceived risks in registrant reviews, examinations, and litigations; and second, to provide economic analysis to support SEC policy development and rulemaking.

There are a few forms required by the SEC that public companies are required to file to give investors a clear understanding of a business' history, progress, and potential future developments. After they are submitted, the SEC analyzes each one to make sure they meet certain requirements. Let's take a glance at each one.

<u>Registration Statements.</u> All companies, whether foreign or domestic, are required to file these unless they qualify for an exemption. The registration statements give investors a better understanding of the profitability and securities of the company and consist of two parts.

The first is Prospectus, which is a legal document that requires the legal entity (issuer) of the securities to give the specifics of the investment that is presented, how the company is being run, its history, financial state, details about its management and insight into any risk. All financial forms, such as the income statement, must be audited by an independent Certified Public Accountant (we will take a further look at this a little later on).

The second is called Additional Information, which is any additional relevant information, such as recent sales of unregistered securities, that must be explained.

The <u>10 – K</u> is a more in-depth financial report. It provides a complete comprehensive analysis of the company, and they must submit it within ninety days of the end of their fiscal year. There are several parts included:

- The Management Discussion and Analysis (MD&A) describes a solid explanation of the company's financial outlook and operations.

- The business summary includes: how the company operates, its history, business segments, research and development, employees, and competition.

- Financial Statements, which are included in the financial report such as the income statement, cash flow statement, and balance sheet.

The <u>10 – Q Report</u> is a shorter version of the 10 – K. This is required within forty-five days after each quarter for the first three quarters of the company's fiscal year. This report offers an overview of the direction the company plans to take and goes into detail about the company's latest developments.

<u>8 – K Report</u> provides any important developments that investors ought to know. However, this form is only submitted if the developments stated didn't make it into 10 – K or 10 – Q in time. The 8 – K addresses specific events and goes into greater detail such as press releases and data tables. Typically, this report would be used in the case of bankruptcy, material impairments, receivership, departures or appointments of executives, completion of acquisition or disposition of assets, or anything else that may be important to investors.

The <u>Proxy Statement</u> is valuable because it informs investors of the company's management's salaries, any perks they may receive and any conflicts of interest that may exist. It must be filed with the SEC before soliciting shareholders' votes on the election of directors and any other approval of corporate actions. Then it is shown before the shareholder meeting.

Investors can watch how purchases and ownerships are shifted based on the decisions made by the company's directors and officers. More specifically, form 3 is the first one that is filed which explains the different ownership amounts. Form 4 dictates any ownership changes during the specific financial period while form 5 shows the information from form 4 in an annual summary.

Schedule 13D introduces the owner(s) to investors while providing contact information and shows who owns the majority of the business' shares. This is filed within ten days of any entity obtaining 5% or more of any class of a company's securities. It also gives background information on the owner including, but not limited to, the relationship type this owner has with the company and any criminal misbehavior they may have been involved with. It provides a detailed explanation about why the operation is taking place and where the money is coming from for the purchase, as well as the type and class of security.

Form 144 shows any pattern of selling securities and gives clues to investors about a corporation's insider pressures to sell. This form stands as a notice of an intent to sell a restricted stock that corporate insiders obtain during a transaction that doesn't involve a public offering. A stock must meet certain conditions before it can be considered transferable and therefore is called a restricted stock. When the amount sold during any three-month period exceeds a certain sales threshold, this form would be required.

Lastly, we have the Foreign Investments. Since 2008, U.S. investors' participation in cross-border securities had stopped due to a rule change. As society has advanced, the SEC has now recognized that technological and global changes have eliminated the requirement for foreign companies without SEC-registered securities to give paper disclosures, resulting in permitting investors to retrieve them online in English. And since companies now have to present them to SEC two months earlier, investors can expect the annual reports promptly.

That was a lot of information, and it can be very tricky to understand each of the statements. It is a little easier to understand the larger picture behind what a company is doing if you can read all of the reports together instead of one at a time. The ability to read between the lines is also going to be important because just like the financial reports, a lot of information can be hidden in unnecessary legal jargon.

Going back, let's re-address a Prospectus because it is important to the issuance of common stock and mutual funds among other securities. You have already gotten the overall concept of what it is, but we are going to go a little further into the details.

This document provides detailed information about a public investment offering for sale. There are three stages. The first is the preliminary prospectus which is provided by the security issuer regarding the first initial offering. It comprises the details of the business and transactions involved, including but not limited to, important information to prospective shareholders about the company's management, description, ownership structure, strategic initiatives, and management. It is filed by a company prior to proceeding with an initial public offering of securities and has been nicknamed the "red herring" because it is required by the SEC to have it be printed with red ink on the left side of the cover.

Once a deal has been made, they would print the final prospectus. This will provide the exact offering price and contains in-depth information about the exact number of shares/certificates that are being issued.

You may also hear it referred to as an 'offering circular' or 'statutory prospectus'. This is the primary source of information investors look for about a publicly offered investment. Concerning mutual funds, this document has the specifics on its objectives, distribution policy, fund management, investment strategies, expenses, fees, and risks.

Not all companies are required to complete this document and can be exempted from filing. In these cases, a company may be offering private offerings to a controlled number of institutions or persons or have offers of a limited size, or securities of municipal, federal and state governments.

To be more specific, a prospectus includes the name of the company that is issuing the stock or the manager of the mutual fund. It will have the type and amount of securities that are being sold, and for stock offerings, a prospectus will include the number of available shares. It advises if the company is offering publicly or privately, the names of the company's principals and how much the underwriters are earning per sale. It always includes a summary of the company's financial information and whether or not the SEC approved it.

The prospectus is a safety net for both the company and investors. It outlines the risks involved for investors about getting involved in a mutual fund or stock with the company. The risks are usually involved early on in the prospectus and continue to be described in more detail later on in the document. It allows potential investors to know the age of the company, describes the capitalization of the stock issuer, and states the amount of management experience and involvement in the business.

There is even a table included that details who owns the stocks, which investors should study to help determine whether the principals are keeping their stock. It is a red flag if you see that the company's shares are being liquidated as it may be a sign of some financial issues within the business. It also protects the company against claims that vital information was not fully disclosed before the investor put money into security.

Quarterly and Annual Reports for Stockholders

You may be wondering the difference between a quarterly and an annual report. So let's take a more in-depth look at both so you can distinguish the similarities and the differences.

A quarterly report is issued by companies every three months. The majority of companies have a financial year that ends on December 31, and quarters that end on March 31, June 30, September 30 and December 31. Some companies, however, have financial years that end at odd times. Apple, for example, has a financial year that ends near the end of September, making their quarterly end dates December 31, March 29 (of the following year), June 28 and September 27.

A quarterly report will include accounting and financial data for the company with details about their gross revenue, operational expenses, cash flow, and net profit. Any company that issues publicly traded shares are required by the Securities and Exchange Commission (SEC) to file an annual 10 – K and a quarterly 10 – Q within sixty days at the end of the applicable period.

The information contained within these two forms alone could include more details than just a quarterly or annual report alone.

A company's management will usually include presentations within a quarterly report with data about key performance indicators and guide analysts and investors. These presentations are routinely followed up by questions and answer periods.

Any analysts that follow a company will often publish their estimates of key metrics (the progress of a company's business goals presented in a measurable value) for future reporting periods. Then, financial publications will average these estimates of a company's earnings per share to arrive at what is called a street consensus. Companies are considered to have beaten the expectations when they exceeded these estimates and companies whose results are below the estimates are considered to have missed the expectations.

Annual reports were not a regular component of corporate financial reporting until the stock market crash of 1929 when legislation was enacted. An annual report is completed at the end of a company's financial year. As previously stated, for most companies the due date is December 31. All public corporations are required to provide this report to shareholders to describe their financial conditions and their operations.

The beginning of the report typically contains information about the company's activities over the past year usually presented as a combination of photos, graphics, and a narrative. Whereas the back part includes details about the company's finances and operational information and will typically include the following sections:

- General Corporate information
- A Letter to the Shareholders from the CEO
- Financial and Operating Highlights
- Narrative Graphics, Text, and Photos
- Financial Statements (including the Balance Sheet, Income Statement, and Cash Flow Statement)
- Footnotes in regards to the Financial Statements
- Auditor's Report
- Accounting Policies
- Summary of Financial Data

These should all be familiar to you already. And although the annual report contains a lot of information about the company, there is an even more detailed report that is called 10 – K.

Since a 10 – K discloses aspects of a fund's operations and financial condition, in the case of mutual funds companies are required to have an annual report made available to the fund's shareholders every fiscal year.

A mutual fund annual report is considered relatively plain compared to a corporate annual report when it comes to its presentation. These reports, along with a statement of additional information and a fund's prospectus, are a source of multi-year performance and fund data which is given to fund shareholders and potential investors. Mutual fund annual reports are considered to be more quantitative vs. qualitative since they address all the mandatory accounting disclosures that are required of mutual funds and typically includes:

- A complete summary list of the holdings (at least the top fifty) and any audited financial statements.

- Tables, charts, or graphs of the holdings by category (geographic region, industry sector, credit quality, type of security, etc.)

- Condensed financial statements

- Tables showing the fund's returns for one, five, and ten year periods

- Management information about the officers and directors, like their names, length of time at the fund and their ages

- Management's discussion of fund performance

- Compensation that is paid to directors and officers

Press Releases and Conference Calls; Why are they Important?

Aside from all of the reports companies are required to file, sometimes a press release or conference call is a good way to get more information about what is going on within a company, financially or otherwise. They may use these outlets as a way to inform the public of a new development like a new product or service or any other material news. A press release and a conference call differ in a couple of ways, so here is a summary about each one.

A press release is a piece of news that companies send out to the public. It will sometimes include information about headline revenue, growth from the previous year or quarter or highlight key financial metrics for the recently completed quarter. Including the key financial metrics would be an example of an 'earnings release'; it will include the company's headline revenue or earnings per share (EPS).

Aside from just the financial figures, they also list valuable contact information such as the company's web address and address information to help investors with their research. The goal is to include all of the essential information (Who? What? When? Where? and Why?) so that journalists or news reports have all the information needed to generate a store and spread the information to the public.

Press releases are produced by the company, not journalists or reporters. These days it can be difficult to distinguish between a story published by a news publication or a press release. However, paying attention to the first few words will usually clarify the origin of the piece.

Companies will issue press releases for a variety of reasons. Many of them do it for the reasons listed above, but for newer businesses, a press release can help establish them within their industry. By becoming established, it helps a company or business gain the trust of their customers; after all, if people trust a company, they are more apt to purchase goods or services from the company. A press release is a great way for a company to announce a new product or partnership. It brings the attention to journalists to cover the story and helps grow their audience.

For anyone wanting to know any financial impact occurring within a company, they aren't going to find it here since the purpose of a press release is supposed to showcase the good, not the bad.

Conversely, a conference call occurs three to four times a year and allows investors to listen to the management of a company discuss the aspects of forwarding earnings growth and what is happening during the current quarter. Usually, these calls are recorded and broadcasted live onto the Internet and have the CEO, senior vice presidents and/or CFO on the call. The CEO may make some generalized comments about the quarter and some big picture future related statements and address any controversy that may have occurred. The goal is for the executives of a company to address specific financial metrics that have impacted their quarterly results, such as revenue growth, margin expansion or profitability. So listening to a conference call is probably going to be more informative than reading or listening to a press release because it may give more insight into what's going on within a company financially.

Press releases and conference calls aren't the only places you can dig for additional information about a company's financial standing. You could try just visiting their website. SEC requires companies to post all of their financial statements or revised financial statements on their websites. The reason for this is so investors can efficiently analyze their financial data and compare it to other companies.

But that is not all; they are also encouraged to post their non-GAAP financials as well and will include an investor presentation (also known as a Roadshow) which is a presentation that is given by an underwriter or manager to try to get potential investors, analysts and fund managers interested and excited.

Roadshows are a series of meetings that happen across different cities where top executives from a company have the chance to talk with their current or potential investors. They can range from just a couple of days within a country to weeks' worth of traveling across the world to financial centers throughout. Typically, the purpose behind them is to give an initial public offering (IPO), where a privately-owned company's shares go public, and investors have the opportunity to buy. Sometimes a company wants to raise money, so they seek out investors to buy new stock due to potentially a private company going to the public. These presentations can be vital and are one of the most prominent key components in an investor's decision to invest in a company.

These reports can be discussed during a conference call and hold valuable information for investors about what is occurring, especially if they were not a part of the roadshow – since these primarily take place in New York, Boston, L.A., and Chicago.

Conclusion

When you are analyzing a financial report, you have many more things to think about and address than just the four documents we broke down. As you can see from the information in this book, the financial report by itself is not the most all-inclusive window into the financial health of a company. There are many aspects and viewpoints to be aware of and reflect on. The ability to create a financial report can be relatively simple depending on the size and industry of a company. Sometimes it is as simple as filling in the blanks. Other times it can be a long, rigorous process that may make you feel like you are going crazy.

It is vital to your success to learn and understand the terminology in the accounting and finance world to make sure you don't get taken advantage of as a potential investor or to ensure you are following the rules and regulations within the dynamics of each report. I stand by what I said at the beginning: most of the legal jargon is unnecessary, but if you can grasp a basic understanding of the terminology, then you will find that you have better success in understanding what is going on in the financial world – not just from reading it, but by being involved in it.

Take what you need from this book to help you no matter what personal goals you have.

If you found this content engaging, then you are in the right field. Some people might view this knowledge as boring, but it is actually imperative to know and very beneficial, whether you are an accounting student, work for a business or have your own, or are interested in investing and thus want to learn as much as you can.

Regardless of the reason behind why you chose to read this book, you should now feel like you have better control over everything related to financial reporting.

There is a lot of information to process and retain, so refer to this book any time you need a refresher or starting base for a project, or just for general interest.

Check out more books by Greg Shields

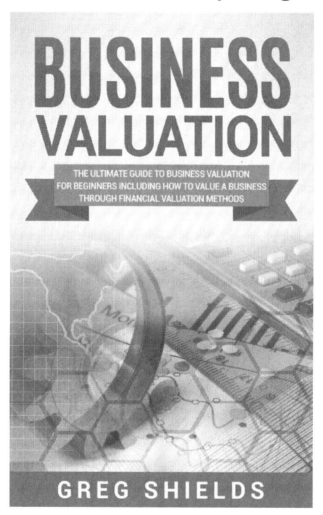

ACCOUNTING

THE ULTIMATE GUIDE TO ACCOUNTING FOR BEGINNERS

Learn Basic Accounting Principles

GREG SHIELDS

Printed in Great Britain
by Amazon